ONE SIGNAL
PUBLISHERS

ATRIA

Goldenrod

Poems

MAGGIE SMITH

**ONE SIGNAL
PUBLISHERS**

ATRIA

NEW YORK LONDON TORONTO SYDNEY NEW DELHI

**ONE SIGNAL
PUBLISHERS**

ATRIA
An Imprint of Simon & Schuster, Inc.
1230 Avenue of the Americas
New York, NY 10020

First One Signal Publishers/Atria Books hardcover edition July 2021

ONE SIGNAL PUBLISHERS / ATRIA BOOKS and colophon are trademarks of
Simon & Schuster, Inc.

For information about special discounts for bulk purchases, please contact Simon
& Schuster Special Sales at 1-866-506-1949 or business@simonandschuster.com.

The Simon & Schuster Speakers Bureau can bring authors to your live event. For
more information or to book an event, contact the Simon & Schuster Speakers
Bureau at 1-866-248-3049 or visit our website at www.simonspeakers.com.

Interior design by Kyoko Watanabe

Manufactured in the United States of America

3 5 7 9 10 8 6 4 2

Library of Congress Control Number: 2021935805

ISBN 978-1-9821-8506-0
ISBN 978-1-9821-8507-7 (ebook)

For my parents
& for my children,
the beloveds who named me

. . . and then I outlived my life

—FORREST GANDER

CONTENTS

1.

3.

1.

This Sort of Thing Happens All the Time

You think you've memorized the calls
of North American birds, particularly

in the East, but one night you hear a call
like a whistle someone is not blowing

hard enough: the ball inside just rattling,
rolling. You see a forested mountain

and dusk is suddenly thick with words,
as if you could hover your cursor

above the pastiche of greens and see
each name pop up: *juniper, citrine, celadon,*

hunter, fern. I'd say *only in a dream,*
but doesn't this sort of thing happen

all the time? One night you find yourself
on a dark street in the suburbs, with air

that smells like cut grass—*jungle*, *myrtle*,
viridian, *spring*—and laundry steam.

You're standing too close to a lit house
which could be yours—is it yours?—

and through blue windows you watch
the evening news. The anchor's mouth

is moving, but outside you hear only
crickets in the cold, dewy lawn.

Crickets and that broken-sounding bird.
Then one dog barking. Then two.

Goldenrod

I'm no botanist. If you're the color of sulfur
and growing at the roadside, you're goldenrod.

You don't care what I call you, whatever
you were born as. You don't know your own name.

But driving near Peoria, the sky pink-orange,
the sun bobbing at the horizon, I see everything

is what it is, exactly, in spite of the words I use:
black cows, barns falling in on themselves, you.

Dear flowers born with a highway view,
forgive me if I've mistaken you. Goldenrod,

whatever your name is, you are with your own kind.
Look—the meadow is a mirror, full of you,

your reflection repeating. Whatever you are,
I see you, wild yellow, and I would let you name me.

Animals

The president called undocumented immigrants
animals, and in the nature documentary
I watched this morning with my kids,
after our Saturday pancakes, the white
fairy tern doesn't build a nest but lays
her single speckled egg in the crook of a branch
or a tree knot. It looks precarious there
because it is. And while she's away,
because even mothers must eat, another bird
swoops in and pecks it, sips some of what now
won't become. The tern returns and knows
something isn't right—the egg crumpled,
the red slick and saplike running down the tree—
but her instinct is so strong, she sits. Just sits
on the broken egg. I have been this bird.
We have been animals all our lives,
with our spines and warm blood, our milky tits
and fine layers of fur. Our live births, too,

if we're lucky. But what animal wrenches
a screaming baby from his mother?
Do we know anymore what it is to be human?
I've stopped knowing what it is to be human.

The Hum

It's not a question
without the mark: How do we live
with trust in a world that will continue

to betray us. Hear my voice
not lift at the end. How do we trust
when we continue to be betrayed.

For the first time I doubt
we'll find our way back. But how
can we not. See how the terminal

mark allows a question
to dress as statement and vice versa.
Sometimes if I am quiet and still,

I can hear a small hum
inside me, an appliance left running.
Years ago I thought it was coming

from my bones. The hum
kept me company, and I thought
thank god for bones, for the fidelity

of bones—they'll be there
until the end and then some.
Now what. How to continue.

I've started calling the hum
the soul. Today I have to hold
my breath to hear it. What question

does it keep not asking
and not asking, never changing
its pitch. How do I answer.

In the Grand Scheme of Things

It sounds like someone wound up the wrens
and let them go, let them chatter across your lawn

like cheap toys, and from here an airplane
seems to fly only from one tree to another, barely

chalking a line between them. We say *the naked eye*
as if the eye could be clothed, as if it isn't the world

that refuses to undress unless we turn our backs.
It shows us what it chooses, nothing more,

and it's not waxing pastoral. There is too much
now at stake. The skeletal rattle you hear

at the window could be only the hellion roses
in the wind, their thorns etching the glass,

but it could be bones. The country we call ours

isn't, and it's full of them. Every year you dig

that goddamn rose bush from the bed, spoon it

from soil like a tumor, and every year it grows back

thick and wild. We say *in the grand scheme of things*

as if there were one. We say *that's not how*

the world works as if the world works.

Ohio Cento

The sun comes up, and soon
the you-know-what will hit the you-know-what.
But this is what it means to have our life.

We need a break from this ruined country.
Sometimes it feels like it has just begun and it's over.

What we know of ourselves
gets compressed, layered. Remembering
is an anniversary; every minute, a commemoration

of being, or thinking—or its opposite,
a strip of negatives.

Some days, I don't even know how to be.
I sink my feet past time in the Olentangy
as if loneliness didn't make us

in some absurd blessing.—If there even is an us.
When are we most ourselves, and when the least?

Is it too late except to say *too late* and hear
the whole world take a rain check?
I worry it is.

Lacrimae

Green dashes for grassland, brown dots
for desert, solid blue for water—

the children's atlas is all simulacra,
from the Latin for *likeness*, which always

reminds me of *lacrimae*, Latin for *tears*.
That's the rickety bridge my brain makes

over the river, or the kinked blue line
that stands for it. What a landscape

in the symbolic distance: dark green
lollipops for deciduous forest,

a cluster of black carats for mountains.
Once, doing dishes, I overheard

my children bickering about metaphysics
in the next room. The three-year-old

said, *Everything is true*, and his older
sister countered, *Do you mean real?*

When I think *likeness*, I think
tears—blue always for water, blue

running through and under everything.

Poem Beginning with a Retweet

*If you drive past horses and don't say horses
you're a psychopath.* If you see an airplane
but don't point it out. A rainbow,
a cardinal, a butterfly. If you don't
whisper-shout *albino squirrel! Deer!
Red fox!* If you hear a woodpecker
and don't shush everyone around you
into silence. If you find an unbroken
sand dollar in a tide pool. If you see
a dorsal fin breaking the water.
If you see the moon and don't say
oh my god look at the moon. If you smell
smoke and don't search for fire.
If you feel yourself receding, receding,
and don't tell anyone until you're gone.

Walking the Dog

If I saw myself walking down Roosevelt Avenue
this morning, what would I think of that woman,

40ish, hauling her dog on a leash—*no, leave it,*
leave it, good girl—her two kids dawdling behind,

found sticks in hand, whining about the heat,
the pavement already silvery? I'd think her left palm—

my left palm—is raw where the leash cuts in,
the terrier pulling, insistent, nose to the ground.

What is she on to? That a scent sliced its way
through this too-thick air is reason enough to

follow it. What is she on to now? I mean the woman.
I mean me. What does she follow by instinct alone?

What does she refuse to be tugged away from,
the woman I hardly know on the street

or in the mirror, hair parted on the wrong side,
pink mole on the opposite cheek? I know the mirror

has something to do with recognition, but today
I think it has everything to do with the critic in me

who cringes to say *recognition*. If I saw myself
walking the dog, seeing is all I could offer. Look,

that's me, coaxing my wilted kids down the block,
the pavement already shimmering like a burn.

Starlings

The starlings choose one piece of sky above the river
    & pour themselves in. They must be a thousand arrows
        pointing in unison one way, then another. That bit of blue
    doesn't belong to them, and they don't belong to the sky,
or to the earth, or to us. Isn't that what you've been taught—
    nothing is ours? Haven't you learned to keep the loosest
        possible hold? The small portion of sky boils with birds.
    Near the river's edge, one birch has a knot so much
like an eye, you think it sees you. But of course it doesn't.

Written Deer

Why does this written doe bound through these written woods?
—WISŁAWA SZYMBORSKA

My handwriting is all over these woods.
No, my handwriting is these woods,

each tree a half-print, half-cursive scrawl,
each loop a limb. My house is somewhere
here, & I have scribbled myself inside it.

What is home but a book we write, then
read again & again, each time dog-earing

different pages. In the morning I wake
in time to pencil the sun high. How
fragile it is, the world—I almost wrote

the word but caught myself. Either one
could be erased. In these written woods,

branches smudge around me whenever
I take a deep breath. Still, written fawns
lie in the written sunlight that dapples

their backs. What is home but a passage
I'm writing & underlining every time I read it.

Rose Has Hands

My phone doesn't observe
the high holidays, autocorrecting
shana tova to *shaman tobacco*,
Rosh Hashanah to *rose has hands.*

Apples and honey for a sweet
new year, or *apples* and
honestly, or *news* and *years*—
always more than one.

Yesterday my daughter asked,
out of what felt like nowhere
but must be a real place
inside her, *When people kidnap*

kids, do they kill them? Why
would someone kill a kid?
When I texted my husband
this, my phone corrected

kill to *Killarney*, *kid* to *kids*.
We have two. My phone suggests
their names. Suggests *what
the duck*. Suggests news, years,

and honestly—what truth
can I tell her? I don't
ducking understand, I don't
understand ducking any of it.

At the End of Our Marriage, in the Backyard

We let the lawn go to wild violets and dandelions,
to crabgrass, to clover bending under the weight

of so many honeybees, our children can't run
barefoot. We do nothing, letting ivy snarl

around the downspouts and air conditioner,
letting milkweed grow and float its white feathers.

We do nothing and call it something—as if
this wilding were intentional. If there is honey,

I tell myself, we are to thank. All summer
the children must wear shoes. We sit out back

while they crouch in the clover, watching the bees,
calling out when they see sunny crumbs of pollen

on their legs. Maybe no one will be stung.
Late in the season, we sit ankle-deep

in weeds and flowers. In weeds we call flowers.

If I could set this to music

with heys & handclaps, with yodels
& banjo & what's the chord

that sounds like what the sun does
to leaves late in the day?

If I could find a melody
you could hum along to, then

handclap, handclap, hey!—
& a banjo part that breaks your heart

the way "Rainbow Connection"
always has, admit it, then what?

Harmonica? Oohs & cowbell?
If I could come up

with a chorus, a bridge,
a harmony & a little slide guitar

rising like a question
you didn't know you needed

answered, I think you would
hear me. I think the music

would slip my words inside
the slats of your ribs—

then handclap, hey!
& sleigh bells & a banjo solo

& there goes the sun again,
strumming & plucking the leaves—

Talk of Horses

Funny, what swims up in the mind:
sample lipsticks, thimble-sized,
that the Avon lady handed my mother
at our front door. We lived
on Lilacwood Avenue. I was four
or five, maybe even younger, eyeing
the pinks, reds, corals the size
of my pinky tip. When we lived
in that house, I remember visiting
my aunt and uncle in the country.
They had cherry trees.
I can see myself under them,
looking up into the branches.
My grandfather lived in the country,
too, in a big house with his new wife—
didn't they have horses?—
while my grandmother rented
a small apartment in the city,
near the shopping mall

where she worked. All these pieces,
what do they add up to? Tiny
lipsticks, cherry trees, talk of horses
I don't think I saw at the house
where my grandfather lived
with his third wife, the one
who seemed so dazed, we secretly
called her *The Spun Pheasant.*
Later my grandfather lost
almost everything in their divorce.
Later my grandmother lost
almost everything in her mind,
but a few memories swam up
now and then to wake her.
All these pieces. If this were
a mystery, we'd consider them clues.
But isn't this a mystery?

Inventive Spelling

There was a lesson I was supposed to learn
but didn't. Years ago. So I'm being taught
again and again, in a language I hardly know.
Whatever it is, I speak so little, I could not go
to a market and buy apples, bread, cheese.
I could not find a hotel with a bed for me,
nor a taxi to take me there. I cannot be
myself in this language, whose sounds
and letters confound me. Inventive spelling
is what we call a young child's translations
from ear to paper, cobbled from consonants
and vowels. When I came home last night
after two days away, my son's markered note
waiting for me on the table looked like this:
evrethenezgoonfin   hopyurhavnagattim
*Everything is going fine here. Hope you are having
a great time.* I'm learning to read his mind

on paper and master more each day. But
the lessons my life keeps trying to teach me—
why still do I misunderstand? Why still
must I keep my eyes down, chalk to the slate?

Stone

Anything the stone knows,
it knows from experience.
If the stone knows touch,
it has the rain's cool lavishing
of attention to thank.
If it knows heat in my hand,
sun-warmed, dry and smooth
as a cheek, then light is where
it can direct its gratitude.
When I close my eyes,
the lids glow. They're learning,
together, to be stones.
What does the stone know
today that it didn't know
yesterday, or the day before?
Violence, too, is a teacher.
The rain drilling a pinhole,
a tiny mouth in the stone,
a tiny ear or eye, over years

is a lesson in patience
but not only patience.
The shoe scuffing it down
the pavement is a lesson.
The stone can be broken
against its brother,
over and over, until together
they dazzle with fire.

Threshold

You want a door you can be
        on both sides of at once.

        You want to be
    on both sides of here

and there, now and then,
        together and—(what

        do we call the life
    we would wish back,

if we could? The before?)
        —alone. But any open

        space may be
    a threshold, an arch

of entering and leaving.
       Crossing a field, wading

              through nothing
      but timothy grass,

imagine yourself passing from
         and into. Passing through

              doorway after
      doorway after doorway.

2.

Slipper

Last time I sat at the sea's open door
I was seven months pregnant,
my son bobbing inside me and the same
roar of waves there. What I love
about the sea is its relentless
newness, the constant turning over—
mornings gray-green, afternoons blue
and glassy, the horizon wearing
its ridiculous white ruff of clouds.
I am becoming my mother here
in a skirted one-piece swimsuit,
my thighs glistening scallop-white
and tender, spreading in the beach chair,
my kids digging broken shells
from the sand at my feet.
My daughter gasps to find one whole—
a common slipper, also called
a boat shell for its shape.
Something once lived there,

something slick and muscular, a tongue
clamped inside. Imagine if I could
wear my home and call it my body,
wear my body and call it home.

For My Next Trick

Where was I, she asks,
before I was in your body?
—What was I?

You were nowhere,
I tell her, *nothing.*

Then where do we go
next? She presses.
Keeps pressing: *Back*

to nothing?
If I could believe

I'll see her again,
waking from whatever
this world is into

another world,
I would—

even if the ending
is so tidy, it spoils
the whole story.

We can't talk
about birth without

talking about death,
can't talk about death
without talking

about separation,
that thick black

redaction.
Do I tell her we end
like a book—*the end?*

That when we're gone,
we're gone, too gone

to miss or even
remember each other?
She knows

what *vanish* means.
Pretending

to do magic,
she says it as a verb:
For my next trick,

I'll vanish you.
I tell her the stars

are the exception—
burned out but still lit.
No, not ghosts,

not exactly. Nothing
to be scared of.

December 18, 2008

For just a fraction of a moment
that afternoon, if we think of time
as being a whole, you were the newest

person in the world. You were
the emptiest vessel on earth,
knowing nothing of this place

or of yourself—that you even were
a self, that a self was something
one could be, that one could be

at all, and what was being?
For that narrowest sliver
of a whole, you were the least

experienced person on earth,
and then you weren't. You knew me
before you knew your own body—

what to do with your hands,
your pink fists battering your face.
We swaddled you as if against

that confusion, though I tell you
that confusion never leaves. The body
remains a house unaware of its rooms.

Small Blue Town

I built a small blue town
inside myself—

blue chapel, blue steeple,
blue houses, blue storefronts,
blue school. A scale model of

a place I've never lived
lives in me. Always

in shadow, the dark blue
of deep shade—
blue rooftops, blue windows,

blue doors. Inside,
you can see it: everything

so steeped in shade,
it's soaked to the bone.
Blue streets, blue lawns,

blue barns in the blue hills
surrounding. The sun

never thinks to rise, to rinse
clear with its light
the small blue town.

Ohio Cento

I began in Ohio
in this town where everyone carries
wavery memory: home,

the sun flatlining the horizon, the wind
to what surely must be another world.

Why does the field begin to ripple
blondes and blondes and blondes?
Perspective can do its thing anywhere.

I had the thought that if I opened up my hand
expecting something casually spiritual,

that if I stepped out of my body I would break.
I mean, yes, we were serious.
Yes. The body's so hard, such awful things inside it.

Expenditure and loss. Collateral and gift.
Yet inside the inside, stillness, if you close your eyes.

Airplanes

My son is safe in bed, the opposite
of gutshot. He is three years old

& wearing new airplane pajamas
with feet & a zipper running

ankle to throat. My son
is sprawled on his back, arms flung

don't shoot wide. This year
I was in none of the pictures

& yet I am in all of them.
That's me, there, the shadow

that shielded his eyes each time
the year shot another

mother's son in the street. No,
not the year. Never the year.

His body is white; it's only his eyes
I have to shield. In the dark

I watch his chest rise & fall,
his lids flicker. My son

is sleeping, covered in airplanes,
& the airplanes are smiling.

Tender Age

America, I've heard the audio:
papa, papa, papa [unintelligible]
[inconsolable crying]

America, my childhood neighborhood
was called Freedom Colony.
I lived on Liberty Lane.

America, you are grand
in theory, poor in practice.
You are not what I learned
in grade school.

America, I'm proofreading
a book on your Constitution.
I'm considering the letter
of the law, the spirit of the law.

America, you've caged
even the babies. They cry
mostly in Spanish.

America, this is you.

America, what I miss most
about church are the hymns—
everyone singing the same word
at the same time. Even the bells
rang in unison.

America, I'm wondering
who your laws serve, the living
or the dead.

America, are there cribs
for the babies? Bars within bars?

America, where does your conscience
live? I mean, from where
has it been removed?

America, as a girl I rode my bike
around the cul-de-sacs: Lexington,
Bunker Hill, Valley Forge.

America, I can pick the stars
and peel the stripes right off you.

America, I'm considering
the letter, the spirit.

America, there is no substitute
for conscience. I can still feel
the bells in my hands.

America, this is us.

America, we have taken children
from their mothers. We have separated
words from their meanings.

America, will there be neighborhoods
named for this undeclared war?

America, where are the babies?

America, when we want to silence
the bells, we extinguish
their open mouths
on our chests.

Prove

I let a thought prove in my head overnight.
In the morning I check to see what's risen.

I try to expect nothing, which is exactly
what I deserve. What kind of woman

demands her head deliver? But sometimes
I wake to a thought doubled, tripled in size

and as good sour as anything grown in the dark.

Poor Sheep

Who sheared the fog
from the mountains?
They're bleating, nearly bald,
huddled together at the horizon.
Or I'm reading too much
into the landscape again.
Projecting, as if playing
a recorded image of myself
on the screen of terrain.
I am transparent and quiet.
You can't quite see me
for the trees, my wet eyes gone
greener than pines. I don't
belong here with these
poor sheep. My skin,
all forest and manifestation
of the interior. You can see
the mountains through me.

Half Staff

Why don't we leave
      the flags at half-staff
& save ourselves

the trouble? Save
      the kids in coats & hats
on flag duty in the snow.

That morning I sat
      in traffic by the school,
waiting for the light

to change, & there
      they were, pulling
the rope hand-over-

hand-over-hand. First
      thought: do children
lowering the flag

at an elementary school
        know it's for children
shot dead at another?

Then the minivan
        behind me honked.
Red to green. So often

I'm reminded the body
        is built for ending.
How have we not

evolved past these
        temporary containers?
I mean, what a place

to keep everything,
        everything! Four days
after Sandy Hook,

I walked my daughter
        to her classroom,
kissed her head,

wished her happy
        birthday, & sent her
inside. So often

the mind whispers
        to the body, *I am not
safe here*, & the body

never bothers
        to answer. Because
what could it say?

Perennials

Let us praise the ghost gardens
of Gary, Detroit, Toledo—abandoned

lots where perennials wake
in competent dirt & frame the absence

of a house. You can hear
the sound of wind, which isn't

wind at all, but leaves touching.
Wind itself can't speak. It needs another

to chime against, knock around.
Again & again the wind finds its tongue,

but its tongue lives outside
of its rusted mouth. Forget the wind.

Let us instead praise meadow & ruin,
weeds & wildflowers seeding

years later. Let us praise the girl
who lives in what they call

a *transitional* neighborhood—
another way of saying *not dead?*

Or *risen from it?* Before running
full-speed through the sprinkler's arc,

she tells her mother, who kneels
in the garden: *Pretend I'm racing*

someone else. Pretend I'm winning.

Interrogators of Orchids

What do we do? We birth the new citizens
& answer their bodies with our bodies.

We rock the new citizens to sleep.
We clothe them with skin & stamp

their passports with milk. We teach
the new citizens to walk & speak.

We show them orchids & ask,
What do they look like? What would you ask

an orchid if you could ask it anything?
We show them wind and light in the trees

& ask, *What does it sound like?*
We hold their hands in our hands

& rub their palms together in small circles
& ask, *Do you hear leaves touching*

each other? We teach the new citizens
to question landscape. We teach them

to love by questioning, & they ask,
Where was I before this place, before

your body, before, before? We birth
the new citizens—interrogators of orchids,

interrogators of air—and bring them
as far as we can. We bring them

to a kind of border, signed & stamped.
The world is a letter we leave them

to steam open. We let them see
dappled shadow under the trees

& ask, *How does light not lose its patience*
between the sky & the ground?

At the End of My Marriage, I Think of Something My Daughter Said About Trees

When a tree is cut down, the sky's like
finally, and rushes in.

Even when you trim a tree,
the sky fills in before the branch

hits the ground. It colors the space blue
because now it can.

Not everything is a poem

or has a poem inside it, but god help me
if I can't find one when I empty

my son's pockets before I do
the wash: one acorn, two rocks

(one smooth and gray, one rough
and glittering, flecked pink),

a chunk of mulch, a wilted
dandelion. The poem is there,

I think, pressing itself against
the grit or splinter or bitter

yellow, but I question its mother-
softness, suspicious of flowers

and laundry. I swear I've seen
poems riding my boy's back

as he runs around our weed patch
of a lawn, letting crabgrass

saw his ankles because killing it
would mean killing the wild

violets, his sister's namesakes.
I don't dare look for poems

in spring even if all the purple
and green are on clearance then.

Two springs ago, my son
was so ill, he smelled bad-sweet,

and one morning he woke
shitting blood, saying my name,

my name, my name. No poem
kept his body from bruising

purple that would fade to green,
his skin a field of flowers—

no, not this poem and not
a poem at all. But he lived.

It's spring again and he lives.
It's spring again and his pockets

are full of petals and stones.

Confession

My son's terrible fevers are softening me
to God. To the idea. When he sizzles

to the touch, speaks a strange new language
of not-consonants and not-vowels, I need

one golden iteration I can live with.
When even syntax is burned black, smelling

of creosote. By nightlight I mitten his hands
and sock his feet with cold washcloths.

I wipe down his cheeks and forehead, his chest
and the back of his neck. He is nearly

too big, but I lift him, hold him guitar-slung
across my body, and sway. Now and then

he whimpers, brain blazing. This is terror
and this must be how it happens—how need

alchemizes into belief. I try to visualize being
held myself, in a cupped hand. In the shining

idea of a hand. I try to feel myself held,
holding. My arms tremble with his weight.

Small Shoes

If there are fewer stars now
than when I was a child,

I can't say
which are missing,
who was the last to see them.

Is it not a crime
unless we call it a crime?

It is difficult to document
a disappearance,
a boat full of stars

capsized.
Stars lying in the sand

facedown,

wearing small shoes.

Add that to the report:

some of the stars washed up

in small shoes.

Planetarium in January

In the coughing, baby-crying
      dark of the planetarium,

                I sit beside my daughter
and draw lines with my eyes

      to connect the stars, to assemble
              the winter sky's falling-down house,

a star-house tipped on its side,
      gables lit, closing in, closer,

            closer—and now I am almost
inside it, almost forgetting

      my daughter beside me,
          the mother and baby

in front of us, and the fussing,

    whispering dark—that teeming

       that can't touch any part of me

in this star-house, this winter

    house I must crawl through because

       it is dark, and because it has fallen.

After the Divorce, I Think of Something My Daughter Said About Mars

Once you go, you can never come back.
If you returned to Earth,

the gravity would turn your bones
to noodles. I mean your skeleton

would sort of melt. So if you go,
you have to stay gone.

Poem Beginning with a Line from Bashō

The moon is brighter since the barn burned.
And by burned I mean to the bones—
the rafters on the ground a whale's rib cage.
A barn is mostly kindling. No wonder
it went up like that—*whoosh*. Or should I
question my perception? As the therapist
tells me, look for evidence to support
the feeling. One minute, beams. The next,
smoke. Didn't my husband say, hardly
to me at all, it was a long time coming?
In this still-smoldering field, I am looking
for evidence. How can something stand
for years, and then—? Just like that?
Where the roof was, all this night.

3.

Invisible Architecture

If I reach my hand out

                in front of me,

if I sweep my arm

            through the air here,

I feel I am touching

            something, slipping

through the invisible

            architecture

around me—

          light erected between

sky & ground,

                city within a city.

Is this faith?

           For years I'd thought

the space around me

           was empty,

waiting for me

           to enter it, to fill it.

The air was a blank

           page I could write on

with my index finger.

                I'd sign my name

near my face, each *G*

                a half-assed

little squiggle.

                I thought wrong.

There is structure

                in the air we move

through. What room

                is this? What hallway

am I feeling my way

                down? What house

have I opened a door to

                & what is held

by this scaffolding

                I can't yet see?

What are they

                supporting, these beams

of light?

Wild

I've talked so much about loving the world
without any idea how to do it.

Something about turning the other cheek?
Something, something, feeding the mouth

that bites you? The world I'm trying to love
is all teeth and need, all gray mange,

but I can't resent the wolf for pulling
the lamb down, even in front of his mother.

I can't be moved by bleating, a limp throat.
The wolf has her own crying young.

I've talked so much about loving the world—
is this how it's done? I am offering

the only thing I have. I am holding out
my hand, feeding myself to the hungry future.

Junk trees,

the Bradford Pears, green-and-white globes of my girlhood
whose smell I've tried to name for years, settling on *piss*,

but walking by a row of them on my way to the grade school,
I thought *baking soda*. Junk trees, those spring debutantes

stinking in their crinoline, begin snowing when the snow
is almost gone—only three more days of cold white once

the forsythia opens its yellow stars, sign of not-quite.
False spring, too, is junk, not science. It serves us right

for asking trees to tell us the time. *Junk trees*, why?
Because they're frail? Because they'll grow anywhere

but not for long? Whatever we call them—bed wetters,
crooked drunks sick on themselves, even semen trees—

they lined the aisles of my growing up, a row on either side
of our street, and threw their rotten white confetti,

smelling of home. And when one failed to thrive,
the city came, dug it up, and planted in its place another.

First Thaw

You must think this house is the world,
the oven door a dark mirror

in which to learn your face.
We've been inside so long, you don't know

a living thing when you see one
through the window: grackles

blacking the dead grass,
sycamores bone-white and eerily

double-jointed. I bundle you
to my chest and step outside, opening

the umbrella. This is the world:
a room that goes on and on—

no walls, no buckling plaster
or cracked ceiling. New as you are,

you aren't the only novice here.
What I thought was a bird—

a large, low-flying white bird—
is a plastic bag. Even the rain knows

only one shape. Look,
it's drawing circles on the puddles.

A Room Like This

I remember best your wild
black hair—how, newborn,
you even had sideburns, even
little lashes on your forehead,
your shoulders. Your round face
a red moon, the kind of warning
sailors know well. I remember
also your low, gruff cry. Bear cub,
you were a growling creature
all your own, not of my body
the way they'd told me
you would be, not an organ
removed, transplanted into air
and fluorescence. I feel
about birth the way I feel
about death: it should not happen
in a room like this, or any room.
I want the smell of soil or salt air,
dark pines, fire and hot stones.

Something elemental.
You should look up and see
not ceiling, at least not
first or last on this earth.
I began this poem thinking
of you, who turned seven
just two days ago, and now
I'm thinking I don't want to die
in a room. It is like my life,
this poem. All this time,
child, I've had no idea
where it's going.

Ohio Cento

Today, summer is slang
a psalmist might have written. I cup in my hands

an idea of an idea
bordered by cornflowers and Queen Anne's lace.

I wonder what this means. I rise into adult air—
the incredible bigness of, you know, all that sky

wealthy with rustling leaves
all over Ohio, gathering a reflection. Of what? Listen.

You hear that bird? Cardinal. Calling his wife
for something to happen. Nothing happens.

Life is funny but not.
The worst things are all true; I have been the girl,

a bird almost—of almost bird alarms,
and then again, and again, and then was gone.

Woman, 41, with a History of Alzheimer's on Both Sides of Her Family

Every night before bed, I lock
the front door, but in the morning
I can't find those metal teeth,
those brassy mountains,

those little saws that lock it
from the outside. I can't remember
what they are called or where
inside I set the memory

of setting them down.
In the night I've jerked awake
to the sound of footsteps
and found it's only springs

creaking in the mattress
when I breathe in, out,
in, out. It's my own filling
and emptying. No one's broken

or entered. I still remember
one night in the beginning
of our brief life together:
the neighbors left for the bar,

and your roommate boosted me
to an open window, climbing in
behind. We took nothing,
only rearranged the furniture.

When they came home
and found everything wrong,
they must have sworn
something was missing.

What Else

The smallest urn I've seen was the size
of my fist. The smallest coffin held
a two-year-old girl and her love-worn
Winnie-the-Pooh. I looked, kept looking,
because how not to? I've forgotten

how to lower my shoulders, how to draw
clean, unbroken breaths from the deep
well of my body, how to unclench
my jaw or else keep cracking my teeth
and tonguing the grit. The smallest

graves I'd see with my eyes closed
but I don't close them. I've forgotten how.
Sleep was a dress I wore threadbare
as a child but grew out of. If there is
a God, is there such a thing

as holy regret for what He's made?
What He's—laissez-faire—allowed us
to break? As if He's turned His head,
watching anything but the world. What else
is there to watch, I want to ask.

Porthole

I was hoping the world would earn you,
but it rains and rains, too busy raining
to win you over. Child, I count ten
rivulets shining down the bedroom wall.

Let's pretend we're on a boat at sea
and watch the neighbor's magnolia trees
pitching through the porthole. The leaves
slosh and thrash against the glass.

Some days I think, *What have I gotten us into?*
This tearstained wall and constant
dripping into buckets, the mold a wild
black shadow. Child, I promise you

the rain will stop. Let's read another chapter
in the book about the kingdom of crows.
It has to stop. Let's count as high as we can
while I braid your bath-damp hair.

Joke

In what I think is a dream,
I look at some manifestation of the past

& say, *I know you're not real.* Someone has to.
And as most dream-things do, the past

shape-shifts, reconstitutes itself with new
eyes & a new haircut—the past

made over—& then I forget its name.
I forget what I'm doing with the past.

What is that joke about the river?
It's not really a joke, no more than past

is really past—the one about water never
being the same water. As it flows past,

the river's current—now *that's* a joke—
is always flowing now, now, now. Past

seven, when I wake from what I think
is a dream—a dream where I tell the past

the truth about itself—it is the present
as it always is. There is no past.

Homesick on a Farm in Franklin, Tennessee

Just outside, in the dark, the shaggy brown pony
and miniature donkeys are bedded down
in the barn. I wonder if the horse whinnies
in her sleep, if the goats are dreaming,
lids twitching over their strange pupils.
And what is a goat's dream? A sweet, untouched
acre of grass? Wind ruffling the salt
and pepper of their coats? The backdrop here
is a mountain furred with bare trees, or a hill
I consider a mountain because I come from Ohio.
Why am I crying? Just this morning a boy
had his birthday party here. I watched
from my cottage window as children held
their hands out, palms flat, to the donkeys.
They fed the chickens, brushed the pony.
Girls cartwheeled across the back paddock.
I watched a boy chase the two pigs—
one round and black, one pink and smaller—
wanting only, I think, to touch them.

During Lockdown, I Let the Dog Sleep in My Bed Again

Last night my daughter cried at bedtime.
Of loneliness, she said. She's seen the graph,
the jagged mountain we need to press
into a meadow, and maybe she pictures
the drive home from southern Ohio,
how the green hills flatten without us
doing a damn thing. No sacrifice required.
I tell her the steep peak makes loneliness
our work, makes an honorable task of it.
But I shut myself in the bathroom and cry, hard,
into a hand towel. I walk alone in the snow,
squinting up into the big, wet flakes,
letting them bathe my face. I tell myself
it is a kind of touch. I tell myself it will do.

Wife for Scale

This is a tender age—and in geologic time,
hardly an age at all. But a golden band

of rock, pressed paper-thin, will stand
for these years, a kind of scientific

shorthand. Once I had a professor
whose wife was in every photo he took

of rock formations. He'd click through
slide after slide, saying: *My wife for scale.*

Isn't there always a woman in the picture
and isn't she always small in comparison?

Forgive me: that was my grief talking.
Tell me: how do I teach myself to be alone?

The strata for this age will not be the first
to reveal what salt does to stone, as if

a sea had been here and not sadness only.
Tell me: with God a question, where

is solace but in the earth? The soil
I'm standing on in this moment—

even as it shifts beneath my feet, as it gives
and cannot hold me—will be rock.

Bride

How long have I been wed
to myself? Calling myself

darling, dressing for my own
pleasure, each morning

choosing perfume to turn
me on. How long have I been

alone in this house but not
alone? Married less

to the man than to the woman
silvering with the mirror.

I know the kind of wife
I need and I become her:

the one who will leave
this earth at the same instant

I do. I am my own bride,
lifting the veil to see

my face. Darling, I say,
I have waited for you all my life.

Talisman

They look like gifts a crow might bring
a human girl, desperate to impress her.
In the left pocket of my thrifted emerald coat:
a scuffed acorn, a glassy black stone,
one pink Mr. Potato Head ear.
When I touch them, I can believe
almost anything. Who's to say
they can't keep me safe? Who's to say
a bird can't court someone's daughter?
But in this life it's my son who shows
his love like a creature that clever,
leaving treasures for my fingers
to worry against. I carry them like
anything I love—until they warm in my palm.
Until I believe. Walking alone at night,
the sky feathered blue-black and slowly
folding over me, I pocket my left hand
and tell myself a story about my life,
a story I call "Talisman," a story
that might end well if I tell it right.

How Dark the Beginning

All we ever talk of is light—
let there be light, there was light then,

good light—but what I consider
dawn is darker than all that.

So many hours between the day
receding and what we recognize

as morning, the sun cresting
like a wave that won't break

over us—as if light were protective,
as if no hearts were flayed,

no bodies broken on a day
like today. In any film,

the sunrise tells us everything
will be all right. Danger wouldn't

dare show up now, dragging
its shadow across the screen.

We talk so much of light, please
let me speak on behalf

of the good dark. Let us
talk more of how dark

the beginning of a day is.

Verse Chorus Verse Chorus Bridge

Until we find the right chord,
>   we can busy ourselves with the lyrics,
>   rhyming not words

but the ideas folded & stacked
>   inside them. Each word unzips its edges
>   & expands to make space

in *copse* for *dusk*, *crepuscular*, *deer.*
>   Room enough for a doe crossing
>   Plumb Road, the rest

hesitating at the shoulder. Room
>   for the little daylight left—we've spent
>   so much already, thinking

there would be more. Each unzipped
>   word, impossibly spacious: room enough
>   in *crepuscular* for *horizon,*

room for the sallow boundary

hours, green-gold, when light is making

a decision. You can see

its thinking happening in real time.

While the right chord searches the air,

we can slant rhyme

what we know now with what

we thought before. We must be coming

to the chorus now.

ACKNOWLEDGMENTS

To my editor, Julia Cheiffetz, and to my literary agent, Joy Tutela: gratitude beyond words. I am the absolute, undisputed luckiest.

To Libby McGuire, Suzanne Donahue, Wendy Sheanin, Dana Trocker, Nick Ciani, Joanna Pinsker, Amara Balan, Liza Buell, Isabel DaSilva, and the whole team at One Signal Publishers and Atria: I am so grateful for your creativity, your expertise, and your dedication. Thank you.

To Anya Backlund, Shannon Hearn, and my Blue Flower Arts family: thank you for taking such good care of me.

To Stanley Plumly (1939–2019), Catherine Pierce, and David Baker: thank you for generous feedback on the individual poems and on the manuscript, and for seeing things I didn't—patterns and possibilities, tangles and snags. Thanks most of all for your friendship, guidance, and care. Stan, you are missed, but you are here—in your wise counsel and in your poems.

To Tyler Meier and Patri Hadad at the University of Arizona Poetry Center: thank you for the time and space. When I arrived in Tucson, I had more than a hundred poems packed in my suitcase. That residency was life-changing.

And to Violet and Rhett: as we say at bedtime, *I love you more . . .* more than all the things, all the words for things, and all the ideas behind the words. I love you more than poems.

CREDITS

Thanks to the editors of the following journals in which certain of these poems first appeared, sometimes in slightly different versions or with different titles:

32 Poems: "Woman, 41, with a History of Alzheimer's on Both Sides of Her Family"

Academy of American Poets Poem-a-Day: "Written Deer"

The Adroit Journal: "First Thaw" & "Slipper"

AGNI: "Walking the Dog" & "Wild"

American Poetry Review: "At the End of Our Marriage, in the Backyard," "Junk trees," "Ohio Cento [The sun comes up, and soon]" & "Small Blue Town"

The Awl: "Poor Sheep"

The Baffler: "In the Grand Scheme of Things"

The Believer: "Rose Has Hands"

Bennington Review: "Invisible Architecture"

Cave Wall: "Tender Age"

Colorado Review: "Poem Beginning with a Retweet" & "Talk of Horses"

Crab Creek Review: "Porthole"

Crab Orchard Review: "Planetarium in January"

The Hong Kong Review: "December 18, 2008" & "Inventive Spelling"

Image: "Confession" & "What Else"

Iron Horse Literary Review: "At the End of My Marriage, I Think of Something My Daughter Said About Trees"

Mississippi Review: "Homesick on a Farm in Franklin, Tennessee"

Narrative: "This Sort of Thing Happens All the Time"

New Decameron: "Not everything is a poem"

New England Review: "The Hum"

The New Yorker: "Bride"

Ninth Letter: "Airplanes"

Plume: "Ohio Cento [I began in Ohio]"

Poetry: "How Dark the Beginning" & "Threshold"

Poetry International: "Half Staff" & "Verse Chorus Verse Chorus Bridge"

Rise Up Review: "Small Shoes"

The Rumpus: "Interrogators of Orchids" & "Stone"

Southern Indiana Review: "Goldenrod" & "Wife for Scale"

The Southern Review: "After the Divorce, I Think of Something My Daughter Said About Mars," "Perennials," "Prove," "Starlings" & "Talisman"

Tin House: "If I could set this to music" & "Joke"

Washington Square Review: "Ohio Cento [Today, summer is slang]"

Wildness: "Lacrimae"

Willow Springs: "For My Next Trick" & "Poem Beginning with a Line from Bashō"

Thank you to the *New York Times* for reprinting "Small Shoes." Thanks to the editors of *Bettering American Poetry* for reprinting "Slipper."

Thanks also to Saara Myrene Raappana and everyone at Motion-poems for including "Small Shoes" in Season 8, and especially to filmmaker Kate Dolan for her beautiful work.

My "Ohio Centos," three of which are included in this book, include lines by poets who were born in Ohio or who were living in the state at the time the cento was written. Grateful acknowledgment to the following poets, not only for their words but for their contributions to Ohio poetry (in alphabetical order): Ruth Awad, David Baker, Mary Biddinger, Elizabeth Breese, Joshua Butts, David Caplan, Barbara Costas, Hart Crane, Patrick Culliton, James Cummins, Dick Davis, Christopher DeWeese, Rita Dove, Kathy Fagan, Noah Falck, Diane Gilliam Fisher, Robert Flanagan, Ross Gay, Mark Halliday, Jeffrey Harrison, Marcus Jackson, Lesley Jenike, Sophia Kartsonis, Kenneth Koch, Dave Lucas, Herbert Woodward Martin, William Matthews, Thylias Moss, Marilyn Nelson, Mary Oliver, Amy Pickworth, Stanley Plumly, Kevin Prufer, Stephanie Rogers, J. Allyn Rosser, Juliana Spahr, Hannah Stephenson, Sommer Sterud, Alison Stine, Eleanor Wilner, and James Wright.

ABOUT THE AUTHOR

Maggie Smith is the award-winning author of *Good Bones, The Well Speaks of Its Own Poison, Lamp of the Body,* and the national bestseller *Keep Moving: Notes on Loss, Creativity, and Change.* A 2011 recipient of a Creative Writing Fellowship from the National Endowment for the Arts, Smith has also received several Individual Excellence Awards from the Ohio Arts Council, two Academy of American Poets Prizes, a Pushcart Prize, and fellowships from the Sustainable Arts Foundation and the Virginia Center for the Creative Arts. She has been widely published, appearing in the *New York Times, The New Yorker,* the *Paris Review, The Best American Poetry,* and more.

 @maggiesmithpoet